Mothers Are a Gift of Love

Helen Steiner Rice

Fleming H. Revell Company
Old Tappan, New Jersey

Unless otherwise identified, Scripture quotations in this book are from the King James Version of the Bible.

Scripture quotations identified LB are from The Living Bible, Copyright © 1971 by Tyndale House Publishers, Wheaton, Illinois 60187. All rights reserved.

Scripture quotations identified PHILLIPS are from THE NEW TESTAMENT IN MODERN ENGLISH (Revised Edition), translated by J.B. Phillips. © J.B. Phillips 1958, 1960, 1972. Used by permission of Macmillan Publishing Co., Inc.

Scripture quotations identified RSV are from the Revised Standard Version of the Bible, copyrighted 1946, 1952, © 1971 and 1973.

Scripture quotations identified NEB are from the New English Bible. © The Delegates of the Oxford University Press and the Syndics of the Cambridge University Press 1961 and 1970. Reprinted by permission.

This arrangement of material was made by Donald T. Kauffman.

Book design and illustrations by John Okladek

Library of Congress Cataloging in Publication Data

Rice, Helen Steiner.
    Mothers are a gift of love.

    1.   Christian poetry, American.   I. Title.
PS 3568.I28M67   811'.54   80-19272
ISBN 0-8007-1135-1
ISBN 0-8007-1136-X (keepsake ed.)

The Love of a Mother

Life's richest treasure
    that money cannot measure
Is a MOTHER'S LOVE . . .
    It is a HEART GIFT FROM GOD ABOVE!

Contents

Love Is a Heart Gift

LOVE is a HEART GIFT
      that cannot be BOUGHT or SOLD
For any amount
      of SILVER or GOLD . . .
And there could never be another
      who LOVES MORE DEEPLY than a MOTHER!

Preface

May memory open the heart's door wide
And make you a child at your mother's side
And may you feel her love around you
As happy memories surround you!

HELEN STEINER RICE

1

No Other Love Like Mother's Love

Mother. No words can ever begin to do justice to the one who bore us and made us what we are. Mother is such a special person! One thing is for sure: There is no one like Mother, no love like Mother's love.

My Love for You

There are things we cannot measure,
Like the depths of waves and sea
And the heights of stars in heaven
And the joy YOU bring to me . . .
Like eternity's long endlessness
And the sunset's golden hue,
There is no way to measure
The love I have for YOU.

Her children arise up, and call her blessed . . . .

Proverbs 31:28

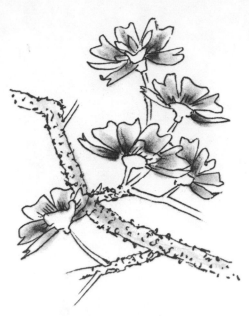

No Other Love
Like Mother's Love

A Mother's love is something
     that no one can explain,
It is made of deep devotion
     and of sacrifice and pain,
It is endless and unselfish
     and enduring come what may
For nothing can destroy it
     or take that love away . . .
It is patient and forgiving
     when all others are forsaking,
And it never fails or falters
     even though the heart is breaking . . .
It believes beyond believing
     when the world around condemns,
And it glows with all the beauty
     of the rarest, brightest gems . . .
It is far beyond defining,
     it defies all explanation,
And it still remains a secret
     like the mysteries of creation . . .
A many splendored miracle
     man cannot understand
And another wondrous evidence
     of God's tender guiding hand.

**As one whom his mother comforteth, so will I
comfort you . . . .**

Isaiah 66:13

Their Love Is All Around You

May the knowledge that YOUR CHILDREN
      and THEIR SWEET CHILDREN, too,
CARE for YOU and LOVE YOU
      "JUST BECAUSE YOU'RE YOU"
KEEP YOU EVER HAPPY
      WHEN LONELY HOURS APPEAR
In KNOWING that THEIR LOVE for YOU
      IS ALL AROUND YOU, DEAR!

Love never ends . . . .

1 Corinthians 13:8 RSV

People Like You

The beauty of God's world
  Is made more beautiful
    By people like you . . .
By the beautiful things
  That you say
    And you do!

A Mother's Love

A *Mother's Love* is like an island
In life's ocean vast and wide,
A peaceful, quiet shelter
From the restless, rising tide . . .

A *Mother's Love* is like a fortress
And we seek protection there
When the waves of tribulation
Seem to drown us in despair . . .

A *Mother's Love's* a sanctuary
Where our souls can find sweet rest
From the struggle and the tension
Of life's fast and futile quest . . .

A *Mother's Love* is like a tower
Rising far above the crowd,
And her smile is like the sunshine
Breaking through a threatening cloud . . .

A *Mother's Love* is like a beacon
Burning bright with Faith and Prayer,
And through the changing scenes of life
We can find a Haven There . . .

For A *Mother's Love* is fashioned
After God's enduring love,
It is endless and unfailing
Like the love of Him above . . .

For God knew in His great wisdom
That He couldn't be Everywhere,
So He put His Little Children
In a Loving Mother's Care.

Give her of the fruit of her hands;
and let her own works praise her in the gates.

Proverbs 31:31

"Flowers Leave
Their Fragrance
On The Hand
That Bestows Them"

There's an old Chinese proverb
    that, if practiced each day,
Would change the whole world
    in a wonderful way—
Its truth is so simple,
    it's so easy to do,
And it works every time
    and successfully, too—
For you can't do a kindness
    without a reward,
Not in silver nor gold
    but in joy from the Lord—
You can't light a candle
    to show others the way
Without feeling the warmth
    of that bright little ray—
And you can't pluck a rose,
    all fragrant with dew,
Without part of its fragrance
    remaining with you . . .

And whose hands bestow
    more fragrant bouquets
Than Mother who daily
    speaks kind words of praise,
A Mother whose courage
    and comfort and cheer
Lights bright little candles
    in hearts through the year—
No wonder the hands
    of an Unselfish Mother
Are symbols of sweetness
    unlike any other.

For Mother
On Mother's Day

No other love
Than mother love
Could do the things
Required of
The one to whom
God gives the keeping
Of His wee lambs,
Awake or sleeping.

Mother's Day

MOTHER'S DAY IS REMBRANCE DAY
And we pause on The Path Of The Year
To pay honor and worshipful tribute
To the Mother our heart holds dear . . .
For, whether here or in heaven,
Her love is our haven and guide,
For always the memory of Mother
Is a beacon light shining inside . . .
Time cannot destroy her memory
And years can never erase
The tenderness and the beauty
Of the love in a Mother's face . . .
And, when we think of our Mother,
We draw nearer to God above,
For only God in His Greatness
Could fashion a MOTHER'S LOVE.

A Tribute To
Colonel John Glenn's Mother
On Mother's Day

When John was just a little boy,
You always found your greatest joy
In watching him from day to day
Exploring "new worlds" in his play . . .
For with a kite string in his hand
He soared into an unknown land,
And with uplifted childish eyes
He tried to penetrate the skies . . .
For little hands and minds reach out
To learn what life is all about,
And God in wisdom and in love
Directs His children's eyes above,
And it was with *Our Father's* grace
That your boy winged his way
through space
And then came safely back to tell—
On earth and sea and sky, as well,
God's handiwork is everywhere
And heaven and earth alike declare
The glory of *"The King of Kings"*
Who gave man all these
wondrous things . . .

And God just chose a man named *Glenn*
To bring *"New Faith"* to "faithless men",
For in this day of automation
Man strives to win his own salvation—
"God's Ways" are something man forgot,
But it took this humble astronaut
To tell the world that faith and truth,
Learned from his parents in his youth,
Have been his shield and armor plate
And gave him strength to penetrate
The vast and wonderful "unknown"
Where all the glory of God is shown . . .
For God never lets His children go
Alone to realms they do not know,
And your son John accomplished more
Than "space programs" were aiming for . . .
He won not just the world's acclaim,
Its plaudits, praise, and hero's fame,
But God looked down upon your son
And softly said . . . *Well Done! Well Done!*
And as the Mother of "the first man in space"
You, too, deserve an honored place—
So on this Mother's Day we cheer
Our choice for *The Mother Of The Year!*

2
Mother Is a Word Called Love

The most wonderful thing in the world is love. Mothers mean so much to us because what they are is what love is—a magic, a mystery, a power that lifts and changes and blesses all it touches. Yes, *Mother* means *Love*.

Mother

YOU'RE THE ANSWER TO
    and THE SYMBOL OF
WHAT IS MARRIAGE
and WHAT IS LOVE!

. . . God is love.
    1 John 4:8

"Mother Is a Word Called Love"

Mother is a word called Love
And all the world is mindful of
The love that's given and shown to others
Is different from The Love of Mothers . . .
For Mothers play the leading roles
In giving birth to little souls,
For though "small souls" are heaven-sent
And we realize they're only lent,
It takes a Mother's loving hands
And her gentle heart that understands
To mold and shape this little life
And shelter it through storm and strife . . .
No other love than Mother Love
Could do the things required of
The one to whom God gives the keeping
Of His wee lambs, awake or sleeping—
So Mothers are a "special race"
God sent to earth to take His place,
And Mother is a lovely name
That even Saints are proud to claim.

**So faith, hope, love
abide, these three; but the greatest of these is love.**

1 Corinthians 13:13 RSV

The Joy of Unselfish Giving

Time is not measured
        by the years that you live
But by the deeds that you do
        and the joy that you give—
And each day as it comes
        brings a chance to each one
To love to the fullest,
        leaving nothing undone
That would brighten the life
        or lighten the load
Of some weary traveler
        lost on Life's Road—
So what does it matter
        how long we may live
If as long as we live
        we unselfishly give.

The Happiness You Give Away Returns to "Shine on You"

The MORE of everything you share,
The MORE you'll always have to spare . . .
For only what you GIVE AWAY
Enriches you from day to day!

A Prayer
for Those We Love

"OUR FATHER WHO ART IN HEAVEN,"
Hear this little prayer
And reach across the miles today
That stretch from HERE to THERE,
So I may feel much closer
To those I'm fondest of
And they may know I think of them
With thankfulness and love,
And help all people everywhere
Who must often dwell apart
To know that they're TOGETHER
In THE HAVEN of THE HEART!

The Gift of Lasting Love

Love is much more than a tender caress
    and more than bright hours of gay happiness,
For a lasting love is made up of sharing
    both hours that are "joyous" and also "despairing" . . .
It's made up of patience and deep understanding
    and never of selfish and stubborn demanding,
It's made up of "CLIMBING THE STEEP HILLS TOGETHER"
    and facing with courage "LIFE'S STORMIEST WEATHER" . . .
And nothing on earth or in heaven can part
    a love that has grown to be part of the heart,
And just like the sun and the stars and the sea,
    this love will go on through ETERNITY—
For "true love" lives on when earthly things die,
    for it's part of the SPIRIT that soars to the "SKY."

Love . . . can outlast anything.

   1 Corinthians 13:7 PHILLIPS

The Magic of Love

Love is like magic
And it always will be,
For love still remains
Life's sweet mystery!

Love works in ways
That are wondrous and strange
And there's nothing in life
That love cannot change!

Love can transform
The most commonplace
Into beauty and splendor
And sweetness and grace!

Love is unselfish,
Understanding and kind,
For it sees with its heart
And not with with its mind!

Love is the answer
That everyone seeks—
Love is the language
That every heart speaks—

Love can't be bought,
It is priceless and free,
Love, like pure magic,
Is a sweet mystery!

Warm Our Hearts With Thy Love

Oh, God, who made the summer
    and warmed the earth with beauty,
Warm our hearts with gratitude
    and devotion to our duty,
For in this age of violence,
    rebellion and defiance
We've forgotten the true meaning
    of "dependable reliance"—
We have lost our sense of duty
    and our sense of values, too,
And what was once unsanctioned,
    no longer is taboo,
Our standards have been lowered
    and we resist all discipline,
And our vision has been narrowed
    and blinded to all sin—
Oh, put the summer brightness
    in our closed, unseeing eyes
So in the careworn faces
    that we pass we'll recognize
The heartbreak and the loneliness,
    the trouble and despair
That a word of understanding
    would make easier to bear—
Oh, God, look down on our cold hearts
    and warm them with Your love,
And grant us Your forgiveness
    which we're so unworthy of.

The Meaning of True Love

It is sharing and caring,
Giving and forgiving,
Loving and being loved,
Walking hand in hand,
Talking heart to heart,
Seeing through each other's eyes,
Laughing together,
Weeping together,
Praying together,
And always trusting
And believing
And thanking GOD
For each other . . .
For love that is shared
      is a beautiful thing—
It enriches the soul
      and makes the heart sing!

Love One Another, for Love Is of God

Every couple should remember
That what the world calls love
Is not something man invented,
But it comes from God above . . .
And love can be neglected
And oftentimes abused,
Perverted and distorted,
Misguided and misused,
Or it can be developed
By living every day
Near to God Our Father
And following in His Way . . .
For God alone can teach you
The meaning of true love,
And He can help establish
The life you're dreaming of
In which you live together
In happiness and peace,
Enjoying married blessings
That day by day increase . . .
For love that is immortal
Has its source in God above,
And the love you give each other
Is founded on His love . . .
And though upon YOUR WEDDING DAY
It seems YOURS and YOURS ALONE,
If you but ask, God takes YOUR LOVE
And blends it with HIS OWN.

When Two People Marry

Your hearts are filled with happiness
    so great and overflowing,
You cannot comprehend it
    for it's far beyond all knowing
How any heart could hold such joy
    or feel the fullness of
The wonder and the glory
    and the ecstasy of love—
You wish that you could capture it
    and never let it go
So you might walk forever
    in its radiant magic glow . . .
But love in all its ecstasy
    is such a fragile thing,
Like gossamer in cloudless skies
    or a hummingbird's small wing,
But love that lasts FOREVER
    must be made of something strong,
The kind of strength that's gathered
    when the heart can hear no song,
When the "sunshine" of your wedding day
    runs into "stormy weather"
And hand in hand you brave the gale
    and climb steep hills together,
And clinging to each other
    while the thunder rolls above
You seek divine protection
    in FAITH and HOPE and LOVE . . .
For "DAYS OF WINE AND ROSES"
    never make love's dream come true,
It takes sacrifice and teardrops,
    and problems shared by two,
To give true love its BEAUTY,
    its GRANDEUR and its FINENESS
And to mold an "earthly ecstasy"
    into HEAVENLY DIVINENESS.

Remember These Words

We are gathered together
    on this happy day
To stand before God
    and to reverently say:
I take thee to be
    my partner for life,
To love and to live with
    as husband and wife;
To have and to hold
    forever, Sweetheart,
Through sickness and health
    until death do us part;
To love and to cherish
    whatever betide,
And in BETTER or WORSE
    to stand by your side . . .
We do this not lightly
    but solemnly, Lord,
Asking Thy blessing
    as we live in accord
With Thy Holy Precepts
    which join us in love
And assure us Thy guidance
    and grace from above . . .
And grant us, dear Lord,
    that "I WILL" and "I DO"
Are words that grow deeper
    and more meaningful, too,
Through long happy years
    of caring and sharing,
Secure in the knowledge
    that we are preparing
A love that is endless
    and never can die
But finds its fulfillment
    with *YOU* in the "SKY".

3
Birthdays Are a Gift From God

On the road of life, birthdays can help us stop and think and look around and thank God. Often we are too busy to see His blessings. Birthdays give us a chance to pause and catch our breath and look up.

Life Is a Highway

LIFE is a HIGHWAY
      on which the years go by . . .
Sometimes the ROAD is LEVEL,
      sometimes the HILLS are HIGH . . .
But as we travel onward
      to a future that's unknown
We can make EACH MILE we travel
      A "HEAVENLY STEPPING-STONE"!

**I will lift up mine eyes unto the hills,
from whence cometh my help.**

Psalms 121:1

Birthdays Are a Gift From God

Where does TIME go in its endless flight—
Spring turns to fall and day to night,
And birthdays come and birthdays go
And where they go we do not know . . .
But God who planned our life on earth
And gave our mind and body birth
And then enclosed a living soul
With heaven as the spirit's goal
Has given man the gift of choice
To follow that small inner voice
That speaks to us from year to year
Reminding us we've naught to fear . . .
For BIRTHDAYS are a STEPPINGSTONE
To endless joys as yet unknown.
So fill each day with happy things
And may your burdens all take wings
And fly away and leave behind
Great joy of heart and peace of mind . . .
For BIRTHDAYS are THE GATEWAY to
An ENDLESS LIFE OF JOY FOR YOU
If you but pray from day to day
That He will show you the TRUTH and
      THE WAY.

My times are in thy hand. . . .

Psalms 31:15

One Thing Never Changes

The seasons swiftly come and go
And with them comes the thought
Of all the various changes
That time in flight has brought . . .
But one thing never changes,
It remains the same forever,
GOD truly loves "HIS CHILDREN"
And HE will forsake them never!

. . . I will never leave thee, nor forsake thee.

Hebrews 13:5

Not by the Years We Live
But how Much We Give

From one day to another
        God will gladly give
To everyone who seeks HIM
        and tries each day to live
A little bit more closely
        to GOD and to each other,
Seeing everyone who passes
        as a neighbor, friend or brother,
Not only joy and happiness
        but the faith to meet each trial
Not with fear and trepidation
        but with an "inner smile"—
For we know life's never measured
        by how many years we live
But by the kindly things we do
        and the happiness we give.

**But the path of the just is as the shining
light, that shineth more and more unto the perfect day.**

Proverbs 4:18

31

Growing Older
Is Part of God's Plan

You can't "hold back the dawn"
Or "stop the tides from flowing"—
Or "keep a rose from withering"
Or "still a wind that's blowing"—
And time cannot be halted
in its swift and endless flight
For age is sure to follow youth
like day comes after night . . .
For He who sets our span of years
and watches from above
Replaces youth and beauty
with Peace and Truth and Love . . .
And then our souls are privileged
to see a "hidden treasure"
That in our youth escaped our eyes
in our pursuit of pleasure . . .
So birthdays are but blessings
that open up the way
To the everlasting beauty
of God's eternal day.

The Golden Years
of Life

GOD in HIS LOVING
        AND ALL-WISE WAY
Makes the heart
        that once was young and gay
Serene and more gentle
        and less restless, too,
Content to remember
        the joys it once knew . . .
And all that we sought
        on "the pathway of pleasure"
Becomes but a memory
        to cherish and treasure—
The fast pace grows slower
        and the spirit serene,
And our souls can envision
        what our eyes have not seen . . .
And so while "LIFE'S SPRINGTIME"
        is sweet to recall,
The "AUTUMN OF LIFE"
        is THE BEST TIME of all,
For our wild, youthful yearnings
        all gradually cease
And GOD fills our days
        with BEAUTY and PEACE!

Life's Golden Autumn

BIRTHDAYS come and BIRTHDAYS go
    and with them comes the thought
Of all the happy MEMORIES
    that the passing years have brought—
And looking back across the years
    it's a joy to reminisce,
For MEMORY OPENS WIDE THE DOOR
    on a happy day like this,
And with a sweet nostalgia
    we longingly recall
The HAPPY DAYS of LONG AGO
    that seem the BEST OF ALL—
But TIME cannot be halted
    in its swift and endless flight
And AGE is sure to follow YOUTH
    as DAY comes after NIGHT—
And once again it's proven
    that the restless brain of man
Is powerless to alter
    GOD'S GREAT UNCHANGING PLAN—
But while our step grows slower
    and we grow more tired, too,
The SOUL goes soaring UPWARD
    to realms untouched and new,
For growing older only means
    the SPIRIT grows serene
And we behold things with OUR SOULS
    that our eyes have never seen—
And BIRTHDAYS are but GATEWAYS
    to ETERNAL LIFE ABOVE
Where "God's children" live FOREVER
    in the BEAUTY of HIS LOVE.

4
A Sure Way to a Happy Day

If people could buy happiness, someone would make a lot of money. While a lot of people keep searching for happiness, it comes every day to those who do the few simple things I suggest in my poems.

How to Find Happiness

Happiness is something that is never far away,
It's as close as the things we do and we say—
So start out today with a smile on your face
And make this old world a happier place.

**And the Lord will guide you continually,
and satisfy you with all good things. . . .**

Isaiah 58:11 LB

A Sure Way to a Happy Day

HAPPINESS is something
    we create in our mind.
It's not something you search for
    and so seldom find—
It's just waking up
    and beginning the day
By counting our blessings
    and kneeling to pray—
It's giving up thoughts
    that breed discontent
And accepting what comes
    as a "gift heaven-sent"—
It's giving up wishing
    for things we have not
And making the best of
    whatever we've got—
It's knowing that life
    is determined for us.
And pursuing our tasks
    —without fret, fume or fuss—
For it's by completing
    what God gives us to do
That we find real contentment
    and happiness, too.

**This is the day which the Lord hath made;
we will rejoice and be glad in it.**

Psalms 118:24

For One Who Gives
So Much to Others

It's not the things that can be bought
that are life's richest treasure,
It's just the little "heart gifts"
that money cannot measure . . .
A cheerful smile, a friendly word,
a sympathetic nod
Are priceless little treasures
from the storehouse of our God . . .
They are the things that can't be bought
with silver or with gold,
For thoughtfulness and kindness
and love are never sold . . .
They are the priceless things in life
for which no one can pay,
And the giver finds rich recompense
in Giving Them Away . . .
And who on earth gives more away
and does more good for others
Than understanding, kind and wise
and selfless, loving Mothers
Who ask no more than just the joy
of helping those they love
To find in life the happiness
that they are dreaming of.

**Give, and it shall be given unto you;
good measure, pressed down, and shaken together,
and running over. . . .**

Luke 6:38

Quit Supposin'

Don't start your day by supposin'
    that trouble is just ahead,
It's better to stop supposin'
    and start with a prayer instead,
And make it a prayer of THANKSGIVING
    for the wonderful things God has wrought
Like the beautiful sunrise and sunset,
    "GOD'S GIFTS"that are free
    and not bought—
For what is the use of supposin'
    the dire things that could happen to you
And worry about some misfortune
    that seldom if ever comes true—
But instead of just idle supposin'
    step forward to meet each new day
Secure in the knowledge God's near you
    to lead you each step of the way—
For supposin' the worst things will happen
    only helps to make them come true
And you darken the bright, happy moments
    that the dear Lord has given to you—
So if you desire to be happy
    and get rid of the "MISERY of DREAD"
Just give up "SUPPOSIN' THE WORST THINGS"
    and look for "THE BEST THINGS" instead.

Surely goodness and mercy shall follow me
all the days of my life. . . .

                    Psalms 23:6

It's Such a Busy World!

Our days are so crowded
     and our hours are so few
And there's so little time
     and so much to do
That the days fly by
     and are over and done
Before we have even
     half begun
To do the things
     that we meant to do
But never have time
     to carry through—
And how nice it would be
     if we stopped to say
The things we feel
     in our hearts each day!

Every Day Is a Reason for Giving—and Giving Is the Key to Living!

So let us give "ourselves" away
Not just today but every day . . .
And remember a kind and thoughtful deed
Or a hand outstretched in time of need
Is the rarest of gifts, for it is a part
Not of the purse but a loving heart—
And he who gives of himself will find
True joy of heart and peace of mind.

**. . . he which soweth bountifully shall
reap also bountifully.**

2 Corinthians 9:6

Every Day Is a Holiday
to Thank and Praise the Lord

Special poems for special seasons
          are meaningful indeed,
But DAILY INSPIRATION
          is still man's greatest need—
For day by day all through the year,
          not just on holidays,
Man should glorify the Lord
          in deeds and words of praise—
And when the heart is heavy
          and everything goes wrong,
May these "Daily Words for Daily Needs"
          be like a cheery song
Assuring you "HE LOVES YOU"
          and that "YOU NEVER WALK ALONE"—
For in God's all-wise wisdom
          your EVERY NEED IS KNOWN!

Seven times a day do I praise thee. . . .
                    Psalms 119:164

Two Palestinian Seas

A very favorite story of mine
Is about Two Seas in Palestine—
❀ ❀ ❀

One is a sparkling sapphire jewel,
Its waters are clean and clear and cool,
Along its shores the children play
And travelers seek it on their way,
And nature gives so lavishly
Her choicest gems to the Galilee . . .
But on to the south the Jordan flows
Into a sea where nothing grows,
No splash of fish, no singing bird,
No children's laughter
is ever heard,
The air hangs heavy all around
And nature shuns this barren ground . . .
Both seas receive the Jordan's flow,
The water is just the same, we know,
But one of the seas, like liquid sun,
Can warm the hearts of everyone,
While farther south another sea
Is dead and dark and miserly—
It takes each drop the Jordan brings
And to each drop it fiercely clings . . .

It hoards and holds the Jordan's waves
Until like shackled, captured slaves
The fresh, clear Jordan turns to salt
And dies within the Dead Sea's vault . . .
But the Jordan flows on rapturously
As it enters and leaves the Galilee,
For every drop that the Jordan gives
Becomes a laughing wave
that lives—
For the Galilee gives back each drop,
Its waters flow and never stop,
And in this laughing, living sea
That takes and gives so generously
We find the way to Life and Living
Is not in Keeping, but in Giving!
❀ ❀ ❀

Yes, there are Two Palestinian Seas
And mankind is fashioned after these!

. . . freely ye have received, freely give.

Matthew 10:8

Give Lavishly! Live Abundantly!

The more you give,
      the more you get—
The more you laugh,
      the less you fret—
The more you do
      unselfishly,
The more you live
      abundantly . . .
The more of everything
      you share,
The more you'll always
      have to spare—
The more you love,
      the more you'll find
That life is good
      and friends are kind . . .
For only what
      we give away,
Enriches us
      from day to day.

**. . . I am come that they might have life,
and that they might have it more abundantly.**

John 10:10

God, Grant Me . . .

COURAGE and HOPE
      for every day,
FAITH to guide me
      along my way,
UNDERSTANDING
      and WISDOM, too,
And GRACE TO ACCEPT
      what life gives me to do.

Begin Each Day
by Kneeling to Pray

Start every day
    with a "Good Morning" prayer
And GOD will bless each thing you do
    and keep you in HIS CARE . . .
And never, never sever
    the "SPIRIT'S SILKEN STRAND"
That OUR FATHER up in HEAVEN
    holds in HIS MIGHTY HAND!

Every day will I bless thee. . . .

        Psalms 145:2

Be of Good Cheer

Since fear and dread and worry
Cannot help in any way,
It's much healthier and happier
To be cheerful every day—
And if we'll only try it
We will find, without a doubt,
A cheerful attitude's something
No one should be without—
For when the heart is cheerful
It cannot be filled with fear,
And without fear the way ahead
Seems more distinct and clear—
And we realize there's nothing
We need ever face alone,
For OUR HEAVENLY FATHER loves us
And our problems are HIS OWN.

5
Enjoy His Peace

Sometimes my life has been so full of things crying to be done, it seemed impossible to keep calm and collected. But I have found that God helps me get things done, one thing at a time, and one of His best gifts is peace of mind and heart.

———————————————●———————————————

In all this world through all of time
    There could not be another
Who could fulfill GOD'S purpose
    As completely as a MOTHER!

But the fruit of the Spirit is love, joy, peace. . . .

Galatians 5:22

No Favor Do I Seek Today

I come not to ASK, to PLEAD or IMPLORE You,
I just come to tell You HOW MUCH I ADORE
      You,
For to kneel in Your Presence makes me feel blest
For I know that You know all my needs best . . .
And it fills me with joy just to linger with You
As my soul You replenish and my heart You renew,
For prayer is much more than just asking for things—
It's the PEACE and CONTENTMENT that
      QUIETNESS brings . . .
So thank You again for Your MERCY and LOVE
And for making me heir to YOUR KINGDOM
      ABOVE!

. . . peace be unto thee. . . .

Daniel 10:19

Inspiration!
Meditation!
Dedication!

Brighten your day
And lighten your way,
Lessen your cares
With DAILY PRAYERS,
Quiet your mind
And leave tension behind
And find inspiration
In "hushed meditation."

**Thou wilt keep him in perfect peace,
whose mind is stayed on thee: because he trusteth in thee.**

Isaiah 26:3

There's Peace and Calm
In the 23rd Psalm

With THE LORD as "YOUR SHEPHERD,"
      you have all that you need,
For, if you "FOLLOW IN HIS FOOTSTEPS"
      wherever HE may lead,
HE will guard and guide and keep you
      in HIS loving, watchful care,
And when traveling in "dark valleys,"
      "YOUR SHEPHERD" will be there,
HIS goodness is unfailing,
      HIS kindness knows no end,
For THE LORD is a "GOOD SHEPHERD"
      on whom you can depend . . .
So, when you heart is troubled,
      you'll find quiet peace and calm,
If you open up the Bible
      and just read this treasured Psalm.

The Lord is my shepherd; I shall not want.

Psalms 23:1

Prayer for Patience

God, teach me to be patient—
    Teach me to go slow—
Teach me how to "wait on You"
    When my way I do not know . . .
Teach me sweet forbearance
    When things do not go right
So I remain unruffled
    When others grow uptight . . .
Teach me how to quiet
    My racing, rising heart
So I may hear the answer
    You are trying to impart . . .
Teach me to LET GO, dear God,
    And pray undisturbed until
My heart is filled with inner peace
    And I learn to know YOUR WILL!

. . . be ye transformed by the renewing of your mind, that ye may prove what is that good, and acceptable, and perfect, will of God.

Romans 12:2

48

The Best Medication
Is Meditation

If your "soul is sick"
      and your "heart is sad"
And the good things in life
      begin to look bad,
Don't be too sure
      that you're physically ill
And run to the doctor
      for a sedative pill . . .
For nothing can heal
      a "soul that is sick"
Or guarantee a cure
      as complete and quick
As a heart-to-heart talk
      with GOD and HIS SON,
Who on the shores of the Galilee
      just said "THY WILL BE DONE" . . .
So, when you're feeling downcast,
      seek GOD in MEDITATION,
For a little talk with JESUS
      is unfailing MEDICATION.

My meditation of him shall be sweet:
I will be glad in the Lord.

                               Psalms 104:34

The Better You Know Him,
The More You Love Him!

The better you know GOD, the better you feel,
For to learn more about HIM and discover HE'S REAL
Can wholly, completely, and miraculously change,
Reshape and remake and then rearrange
Your mixed-up, miserable, and unhappy life
"Adrift on the sea of sin-sickened strife"—
But when you once know this "MAN OF GOOD WILL,"
HE will calm your life and say "PEACE, BE STILL" . . .
So open your "heart's door" and let CHRIST come in
And HE'LL give you new life and free you from sin—
And there is no joy that can ever compare
With the joy of knowing you're in GOD'S care.

**. . . in every thing by prayer and supplication
with thanksgiving let your requests be made known
unto God. And the peace of God, which passeth all
understanding, shall keep your hearts
and minds through Christ Jesus.**

Philippians 4:6, 7

Peace Begins in the Home
and the Heart

Peace is not something you fight for
With bombs and missiles that kill,
Nor can it be won in a "battle of words"
Man fashions by scheming and skill . . .
For men who are greedy and warlike,
Whose avarice for power cannot cease,
Can never contribute in helping
To bring this world nearer to peace . . .
For in seeking PEACE for ALL PEOPLE
There is only one place to begin
And that is in each HOME and HEART—
For the FORTRESS of PEACE is WITHIN!

He Asks So Little
and
Gives So Much

What must I do
      to insure peace of mind?
Is the answer I'm seeking,
      too hard to find?
How can I know
      what God wants me to be?
How can I tell
      what's expected of me?
Where can I go
      for guidance and aid
To help me correct
      the errors I've made?
The answer is found
      in doing *three things*
And great is the gladness
      that doing them brings . . .
"Do justice"—"Love kindness"—
      "Walk humbly with God"—
For with these *three things*
      as your "rule and your rod"
All things worth having
      are yours to achieve
If you follow God's words
      and have *faith* to *believe*!

6
Climb 'til Your
Dream Comes True

Mothers are dreamers. They have big dreams for their children, often making unbelievable sacrifices to make a dream come true for a son or daughter. But they often have special dreams of their own, and to every mother and everyone who reads this, I say: "Climb 'til your dream comes true!"

"With God
All Things Are Possible!"

Nothing is ever too hard to do
If your FAITH is STRONG and your PURPOSE is TRUE . . .
So "NEVER GIVE UP" and NEVER STOP
Just "JOURNEY ON to THE MOUNTAINTOP"!

. . . all things are possible to him that believeth.

Mark 9:23

"Climb 'Til
Your Dream Comes True"

Often your tasks will be many,
And more than you think you can do . . .
Often the road will be rugged
And the hills insurmountable, too . . .
But always remember,
the hills ahead
Are never as steep as they seem,
And with Faith in your heart
start upward
And climb 'til you reach your dream,
For nothing in life that is worthy
Is ever too hard to achieve
If you have the courage to try it
And you have the Faith to believe . . .
For Faith is a force that is greater
Than knowledge or power
or skill
And many defeats turn to triumph
If you trust in God's wisdom and will . . .
For Faith is a mover of mountains,
There's nothing that God cannot do,
So start out today
with Faith in your heart
And "Climb 'Til Your Dream Comes True"!

. . . with God all things are possible.

Matthew 19:26

Ideals Are Like Stars

In this world of casual carelessness
it's discouraging to try
To keep our morals and standards
and our Ideals High . . .
We are ridiculed and laughed at
by the smart sophisticate
Who proclaims in brittle banter
that such things are
out of date . . .
But no life is worth the living
unless it's built on truth,
And we lay our life's foundation
in the golden years of youth . . .
So allow no one to stop you
or hinder you from laying
A firm and strong foundation
made of Faith and Love
and Praying . . .
And remember that Ideals
are like Stars Up In The Sky,
You can never really reach them,
hanging in the heavens high . . .

But like the mighty mariner
who sailed the storm-tossed sea,
And used the Stars To Chart
His Course
with skill and certainty,
You too can Chart Your Course in Life
With High Ideals and Love,
For High Ideals are like the Stars
that light the sky above . . .
You cannot ever
reach them,
but Lift Your Heart Up High
And your Life will be as Shining
as the Stars Up In The Sky.

He giveth power. . . .
Isaiah 40:29

God's Stairway

Step by step we climb day by day
Closer to God with each prayer we pray
For "the cry of the heart" offered in prayer
Becomes just another "SPIRITUAL STAIR"
In the "HEAVENLY STAIRCASE" leading us to
A beautiful place where we live anew . . .
So never give up for it's worth the climb
To live forever in "ENDLESS TIME"
Where the soul of man is SAFE and FREE
To LIVE IN LOVE THROUGH ETERNITY!

And he dreamed, and behold a ladder set up on the earth, and the top of it reached to heaven: and behold the angels of God ascending and descending on it.

Genesis 28:12

The Praying Hands

The "Praying Hands" are much, much more
    than just a work of art,
They are the "soul's creation"
    of a deeply thankful heart—
They are a Priceless Masterpiece
    that love alone could paint,
And they reveal the selflessness
    of an unheralded saint—
Those hands so scarred and toilworn,
    tell the story of a man
Who sacrificed his talent
    in accordance with God's Plan—
For in God's Plan are many things
    man cannot understand,
But we must trust God's judgment
    and be guided by His Hand—
Sometimes He asks us to give up
    our dreams of happiness,
Sometimes we must forego our hopes
    of fortune and success—
Not all of us can triumph
    or rise to heights of fame,
And many times What Should Be Ours,
    goes to Another Name—

But he who makes a sacrifice,
    so another may succeed,
Is indeed a true disciple
    of our blessed Saviour's creed—
For when we "give ourselves away"
    in sacrifice and love,
We are "laying up rich treasures"
    in God's kingdom up above—
And hidden in gnarled, toilworn hands
    is the truest Art of Living,
Achieved alone by those who've learned
    the "Victory of Giving"—
For any sacrifice on earth,
    made in the dear Lord's name,
Assures the giver of a place
    in Heaven's Hall of Fame—
And who can say with certainty
    Where the Greatest Talent Lies,
Or Who Will Be the Greatest
    In Our Heavenly Father's Eyes!

**. . . for he that is least among you
all, the same shall be great.**

Luke 9:48

Trouble Is a Steppingstone
To Growth

Trouble is something no one can escape,
Everyone has it in some form or shape—
Some people hide it way down deep inside,
Some people bear it with gallant-like pride,
Some people worry and complain of their lot,
Some people covet what they haven't got,
While others rebel and become bitter and old
With hopes that are dead and hearts that are cold . .
But the wise man accepts whatever God sends,
Willing to yield like a storm-tossed tree bends,
Knowing that God never makes a mistake,
So whatever He sends they are willing to take—
For trouble is part and parcel of life
And no man can grow without trouble and strife,
And the steep hills ahead and high mountain peaks
Afford man at last the peace that he seeks—
So blest are the people who learn to accept
The trouble men try to escape and reject,
For in OUR ACCEPTANCE
        we're given great grace
And courage and faith and the strength to face
The daily troubles that come to us all
So we may learn to stand "straight and tall"—
For the grandeur of life is born of defeat
For in overcoming we make life complete.

He that overcometh shall inherit all things. . . .

Revelation 21:7

Burdens Are Things
God Turns Into Wings

"Oh for the wings of a bird," we cry,
To carry us off to an untroubled sky
Where we can dwell untouched by care
And always be free as a bird in the air—
But there is a legend that's very old,
Not often heard and seldom told,
That once all birds were wingless, too,
Unable to soar through the skies of blue—
For, while their plumage was beautifully bright
And their chirping songs were liltingly light,
They, too, were powerless to fly
Until one day when the Lord came by
And laid at the feet of the singing birds
Gossamer wings as He spoke these words:
"Come take these burdens, so heavy now,
But if you bear them you'll learn somehow
That as you wear them they'll grow light
And soon you can lift yourself into flight"—
So folding the wings beneath their hearts,
And after endless failures and starts,
They lifted themselves and found with delight
The wings that were heavy had grown so light—
So let us, too, listen to God's wise words,
For we are much like the "wingless birds,"
And if we would shoulder our daily trials
And learn to wear them with sunny smiles
We'd find they were wings that God had sent
To lift us above our heart's discontent—
For THE WINGS that LIFT us out of despair
Are made by God from the weight of care,
So whenever you cry for "the wings of a bird"
Remember this little legend you've heard
And let God give you a heart that sings
As He turns your burdens to "silver wings."

7
A Friend Is a Gift of God

One of God's greatest blessings is the priceless gift of friendship. My feelings about friends are expressed in a number of poems. Those that follow begin with a very special tribute to a very special person—"Mom"— Ida Lee Ginn, who for many years took care of my every need and was a real mother to me in many, many ways.

———————————————●———————————————

EVERYONE NEEDS SOMEONE
     to be THANKFUL FOR . . .
And each day of life
     we are aware of this more . . .
For the JOY of ENJOYING
     and the FULLNESS of LIVING
Are found ONLY IN HEARTS
     that are filled with THANKSGIVING!

A friend loveth at all times. . . .

       Proverbs 17:17

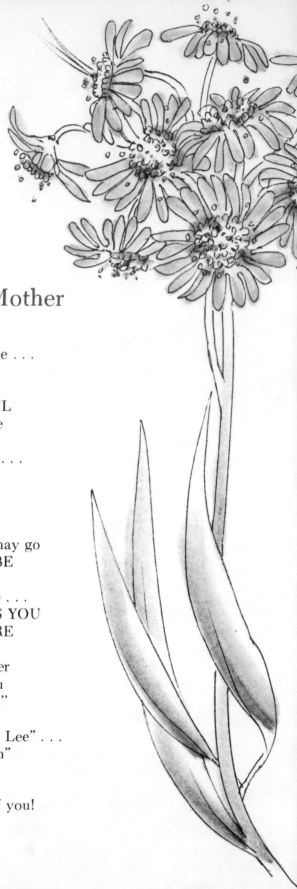

To a Very Special Mother

There is no way to tell you
       how much you mean to me . . .
I only know I'm THANKFUL
       that God sent me Ida Lee,
And I only know I'm GRATEFUL
       that Our Father Up Above
Made You "My Guardian Angel"
       and gave me you to Love . . .
And just between the two of us,
       each time I look at you,
I can't Believe "My Pretty Mom"
       is really EIGHTY-TWO,
For years may come and years may go
       but you WILL ALWAYS BE
The Same Dear Little Lady
       Mr. Braden brought to me . . .
Now may the Good Lord BLESS YOU
       and Keep you in HIS CARE
And I will ask Him every day
       when I go to Him in prayer
That when He gently calls to you
       and says, "Come unto Me,"
He'll also say to Helen Rice,
       "You come along with Ida Lee" . . .
And that will be a "Glad Reunion"
       when I introduce you to
My darling "Little Mother"
       who reminds me, Dear, of you!

A Friend
Is a Gift of God

Among the great and glorious gifts
       our heavenly Father sends
Is the GIFT of UNDERSTANDING
       that we find in loving friends,
For in this world of trouble
       that is filled with anxious care
Everybody needs a friend
       in whom they're free to share
The little secret heartaches
       that lay heavy on their mind,
Not just a mere acquaintance
       but someone who's "JUST OUR KIND"—
For, somehow, in the generous heart
       of loving, faithful friends
The good God in His charity
       and wisdom always sends
A sense of understanding
       and the power of perception
And mixes these fine qualities
       with kindness and affection
So when we need some sympathy
       or a friendly hand to touch,
Or an ear that listens tenderly
       and speaks words that mean so much,
We seek our true and trusted friend
       in the knowledge that we'll find
A heart that's sympathetic
       and an understanding mind . . .
And often just without a word
       there seems to be a union
Of thoughts and kindred feelings
       for GOD gives TRUE FRIENDS communion.

. . . This is my beloved, and this is my friend. . . .

Song of Solomon 5:16

We All Need Somebody

And SOMEBODY like YOU
    can "turn the trick,"
For our lives are empty
    and our world is "sick" . . .
We have lost our morals
    and our principles, too,
And with no purpose in life
    we are lonely and blue . . .
We need SOMEBODY very much
    who has a warm and friendy touch
To make us suddenly aware
    that there are those WHO REALLY CARE!

The Flower of Friendship

LIFE is like a GARDEN
And FRIENDSHIP like a FLOWER
That blooms and grows in beauty
With the sunshine and the shower . . .
And lovely are the blossoms
That are tended with great care
By those who work unselfishly
To make the place more fair . . .
And, like the GARDEN blossoms,
FRIENDSHIP'S FLOWER grows more sweet
When watched and tended carefully
By those we know and meet . . .
And, like sunshine adds new fragrance
And raindrops play their part,
Joy and sadness add new beauty
When there's FRIENDSHIP in the heart . . .
And, if the seed of FRIENDSHIP
Is planted deep and true
And watched with understanding,
FRIENDSHIP'S FLOWER WILL BLOOM FOR YOU.

The Golden Chain Of Friendship

Friendship is a Golden Chain,
The links are friends so dear,
And like a rare and precious jewel
It's treasured more each year . . .
It's clasped together firmly
With a love that's deep and true,
And it's rich with happy memories
And fond recollections, too . . .
Time can't destroy its beauty
For, as long as memory lives,
Years can't erase the pleasure
That the joy of friendship gives . . .
For friendship is a priceless gift
That can't be bought or sold,
But to have an understanding friend
Is worth far more than gold . . .
And the Golden Chain of Friendship
Is a strong and blessed tie
Binding kindred hearts together
As the years go passing by.

Two are better than one. . . .

Ecclesiastes 4:9

Widen My Vision

God, open my eyes
     so I may see
And feel Your presence
     close to me . . .
Give me strength
     for my stumbling feet
As I battle the crowd
     on life's busy street,
And widen my vision
     of my unseeing eyes
So in passing faces
     I'll recognize
Not just a stranger,
     unloved and unknown,
But a friend with a heart
     that is much like my own . . .
Give me perception
     to make me aware
That scattered profusely
     on life's thoroughfare
Are the best GIFTS of GOD
     that we daily pass by
As we look at the world
     with an UNSEEING EYE.

My God Is No Stranger

I've never seen God,
      but I know how I feel,
It's people like You
      who make Him "So Real" . . .
My God is no stranger,
      He's friendly and gay
And He doesn't ask me
      to weep when I pray . . .
It seems that I pass Him
      so often each day
In the faces of people
      I meet on my way . . .
He's the stars in the heaven,
      a smile on some face,
A leaf on a tree
      or a rose in a vase . . .
He's winter and autumn
      and summer and spring,
In short, God Is Every
      Real, Wonderful Thing . . .
I wish I might meet Him
      much more than I do,
I would if there were
      More People Like You.

8
God Loves You

You know what love is, Mother, because your very name is a word for love. The love of God has poured through your life into other lives.

Yes, God has given His love through you. But I want you to know how much *God loves you*.

———————————————●———————————————

The Reflections of God

The silent stars in timeless skies,
The wonderment in children's eyes,
The autumn haze, the breath of spring,
The chirping song the crickets sing,
A rosebud in a slender vase
Are all reflections of GOD's FACE.

We love him, because he first loved us.

1 John 4:19

Where There Is Love

Where there is love the heart is light,
Where there is love the day is bright,
Where there is love there is a song
To help when things are going wrong . . .
Where there is love there is a smile
To make all things seem more worthwhile,
Where there is love there's quiet peace,
A tranquil place where turmoils cease . . .
Love changes darkness into light
And makes the heart take "wingless flight" . . .
And Mothers have a special way
Of filling homes with love each day,
And when the home is filled with love
You'll always find God spoken of,
And when a family "prays together"
That family also "stays together" . . .
And once again a Mother's touch
Can mold and shape and do so much
To make this world a better place
For every color, creed and race—
For when man walks with God again,
There shall be Peace on Earth for Men.

**Love is patient; love is kind . . . .
There is nothing love cannot face; there is no
limit to its faith, its hope, and its endurance.**

1 Corinthians 13:4, 7 NEB

70

Someone Cares

Someone cares and always will,
The world forgets but God loves you still,
You cannot go beyond His Love
No matter what you're guilty of—
For God forgives until the end,
He is your faithful, loyal friend,
And though you try to hide your face
There is no shelter any place
That can escape His watchful eye,
For on the earth and in the sky
HE'S EVER PRESENT and ALWAYS THERE
To take you in His tender care
And bind the wounds and mend the breaks
When all the world around forsakes . . .
SOMEONE CARES and LOVES YOU STILL
And GOD is THE SOMEONE who always will.

Casting all your care upon him; for he careth for you.

1 Peter 5:7

My God Is No Stranger

God is no stranger in a faraway place,
He's as close as the wind that blows cross my face,
It's true I can't see the wind as it blows
But I feel it around me and my heart surely knows
That God's mighty Hand can be felt every minute
For there is nothing on earth that God isn't in it—
The sky and the stars, the waves and the sea,
The dew on the grass, the leaves on a tree
Are constant reminders of God and His nearness,
Proclaiming His Presence with crystal-like clearness—
So how could I think God was far, far away
When I feel Him beside me every hour of the day,
And I've plenty of reasons to know God's My Friend
And this is one Friendship that time cannot end!

. . . lo, I am with you alway. . . .

Matthew 28:20

God Is Everywhere

We cannot go beyond GOD'S reach
or beyond HIS love and care,
For we are all a PART of GOD
and GOD is EVERYWHERE!

The Power of Love

There is no thinking person
who can stand untouched today
And view the world around us
drifting downward to decay
Without feeling deep within them
a silent unnamed dread,
Wondering how to stem the chaos
that lies frightfully ahead . . .
But the problems we are facing
cannot humanly be solved
For our diplomatic strategy
only gets us more involved
And our skillful ingenuity,
our technology and science
Can never change a sinful heart
filled with hatred and defiance . . .
So our problems keep on growing
every hour of every day
As man vainly tries to solve them
in his own SELF-WILLFUL WAY . . .
But man is powerless alone
to CLEAN UP THE WORLD OUTSIDE
Until his own polluted soul
is CLEAN and FREE INSIDE . . .
For the amazing power of love
is beyond all comprehension
And it alone can heal this world
of its hatred and dissension.

. . . let us love one another: for love is of God. . . .

1 John 4:7

72

The Miracle of Miracles . . .

is that God loves YOU and He loves me, too . . .
and through His love, I can share with you . . .
His words which I use in the poems I write . . .
for "He is The Way and The Truth and The
        Light" . . .
And then through His love we communicate . . .
for we work as a blessed TRIUMVIRATE . . .
For my work is a "partnership of THREE" . . .
GOD first, then YOU, and last of all, me . . .
For nothing I write is outstanding or great . . .
until it is "PART of HIS TRIUMVIRATE" . . .
And at Christmas I reach across TIME and
        SPACE . . .
to share GOD'S LOVE and His marvelous
        GRACE . . .
And though we are selfish and sinful and
        small . . .
"HIS GRACE IS SUFFICIENT" to shelter
        us all.

. . . My grace is sufficient for thee. . . .

2 Corinthians 12:9

God's Presence Is
Ever Beside You

And so today I walk with GOD
Because I love HIM so . . .
If I have FAITH and TRUST in HIM,
There's nothing I need know!

Fulfillment

APPLE BLOSSOMS bursting wide
        now beautify the tree
And make a Springtime picture
        that is beautiful to see . . .
Oh, fragrant lovely blossoms,
        You'll make a bright bouquet
If I but break your branches
        from the apple tree today . . .
But if I break your branches
        and make your beauty mine,
You'll bear no fruit in season
        when severed from the vine . . .
And when we cut ourselves away
        from guidance that's divine,
Our lives will be as fruitless
        as the branch without the vine . . .
For as the flowering branches
        depend upon the tree
To nourish and fulfill them
        till they reach futurity,
We too must be dependent
        on our Father up above,
For we are but the BRANCHES
        and He's THE TREE OF LOVE.

"Love Divine, All Love Excelling"

In a myriad of miraculous ways
GOD shapes our lives and changes our days,
Beyond our will or even knowing
GOD keeps our spirit ever growing . . .
For LIGHTS and SHADOWS, SUN and RAIN,
SADNESS and GLADNESS, JOY and PAIN,
Combine to make our lives complete
And give us VICTORY through DEFEAT . . .
"Oh, Love Divine, All Love Excelling,"
In troubled hearts YOU just keep dwelling,
Patiently waiting for a "PRODIGAL SON"
To say at last, "THY WILL BE DONE."

"Seek Ye First
the Kingdom of God"

Always remember
        that whatever betide you
THE POWER of GOD
        is always beside you,
And if friends disappoint you
        and plans go astray
And nothing works out
        in just the right way
And you feel you have failed
        in achieving your goal
And that life wrongly placed you
        in an unfitting role,
Take heart and "stand tall"
        and think who you are,
For GOD is YOUR FATHER
        and no one can bar
Or keep you from reaching
        your desired success
Or withhold the joy
        that is yours to possess . . .
For with GOD on your side
        it matters not who
Is working to keep
        life's good things from you,
For you need nothing more
        than GOD'S GUIDANCE and LOVE
To insure you the things
        that you're most worthy of . . .
So trust in HIS WISDOM
        and follow HIS WAYS
And be not concerned
        with the world's empty praise,
But SEEK FIRST HIS KINGDOM
        and you will possess
The world's greatest riches
        which is true happiness.

God's Assurance
Gives Us Endurance

My blessings are so many,
My troubles are so few,
How can I feel discouraged
When I know that I have YOU
And I have the "SWEET ASSURANCE"
That I'll never stand alone
If I but keep remembering
I am YOURS and YOURS ALONE . . .
So, in this world of trouble
With "darkness" all around,
Take my hand and lead me
Until I stand on "HIGHER GROUND"
And help me to endure the "storms"
That keep raging deep inside me
And make me more aware each day
That no evil can betide me
If I remain undaunted
Though the "billows sweep and roll,"
Knowing I have YOUR ASSURANCE
There's a HAVEN for MY SOUL,
For ANYTHING and EVERYTHING
Can somehow be endured
If YOUR PRESENCE is beside me
And LOVINGLY ASSURED!

9

Learn to Rest so Your Life Will Be Blessed

It is easy to get so overwhelmed with our work or our problems that, even when we are resting, we can't rest. I have found, though, that it is possible to *learn* to rest . . . and be blessed.

We Never Walk Alone

What more can we ask of the SAVIOUR
Than to know we are never alone—
That HIS MERCY and LOVE are unfailing
And HE makes all our problems HIS OWN.

There remaineth therefore a rest to the people of God.

Hebrews 4:9

Learn to Rest
So Your Life Will Be Blest

We all need "short vacations"
        in life's fast and maddening race—
An interlude of quietness
        from the constant, jet-age pace . . .
So, when your day is pressure-packed
        and your hours are all too few,
Just close your eyes and meditate
        and let GOD talk to you,
For, when we keep on pushing,
        we're not following in GOD'S WAY—
We are foolish, selfish robots
        mechanized to fill each day
With unimportant trivia
        that makes life more complex
And gives us greater problems
        to irritate and vex . . .
So, when your nervous network
        becomes a tangled mess,
Just close your eyes in silent prayer
        and ask THE LORD to bless
Each thought that you are thinking,
        each decision you must make,
As well as every word you speak
        and every step you take,
For only by the grace of GOD
        can we gain self-control
And only meditative thoughts
        can restore your "PEACE OF SOUL."

And God is able to make all grace abound toward you. . . .
                      2 Corinthians 9:8

Build a Firm
Foundation of Faith

FAITH is a force that is greater
Than knowledge or power or skill . . .
And the darkest defeat turns to triumph
If we trust in GOD'S WISDOM and WILL.

Put Your Problem in
God's Hands, for He
Completely Understands

Although it sometimes seems to us
      our prayers have not been heard,
GOD always knows our every need
      without a single word . . .
And HE will not forsake us
      even though the way seems steep,
For always HE is near to us
      a tender watch to keep . . .
And in good time HE'LL answer us
      and in HIS love HE'LL send
GREATER THINGS THAN WE HAVE ASKED
      and BLESSINGS WITHOUT END . . .
So though we do not understand
      why trouble comes to man
Can we not be contented
      just to know that IT'S GOD'S PLAN.

**Now unto him that is able to do exceeding abundantly
above all that we ask or think . . . . Unto him be glory. . . .**

Ephesians 3:20, 21

81

Be of Good Cheer—
There's Nothing to Fear!

Cheerful thoughts like sunbeams
Lighten up the "darkest fears"
For when the heart is happy
There's just no time for tears—
And when the face is smiling
It's impossible to frown
And when you are "high-spirited"
You cannot feel "low-down"—
For the nature of our attitude
Toward circumstantial things
Determines our acceptance
Of the problems that life brings.
And since fear and dread and worry
Cannot help in any way,
It's much healthier and happier
To be cheerful every day—
And if you'll only try it
You will find, without a doubt,
A cheerful attitude's something
No one should be without—
For when the heart is cheerful
It cannot be filled with fear.
And without fear the way ahead
Seems more distinct and clear—
And we realize there's nothing
We need ever face alone
For our HEAVENLY FATHER loves us
And our problems are His own.

**For I the Lord thy God will hold
thy right hand, saying unto thee,
Fear not; I will help thee.**

Isaiah 41:13

Anxious Prayers

When we are deeply disturbed with a problem
And our mind is filled with doubt
And we struggle to find a solution
But there seems to be no way out,
We futilely keep on trying
To untangle our web of distress—
But our own little, puny efforts
Meet with very little success . . .
And finally exhausted and weary,
Discouraged and downcast and low,
With no foreseeable answer
And with no other place to go,
We kneel down in sheer desperation
And slowly and stumblingly pray
Then impatiently wait for an answer
Which we fully expect right away . . .
And then, when GOD does not answer,
In one, sudden instant we say,
"GOD does not seem to be listening,
So why should we bother to pray" . . .
But GOD can't get through to "THE ANXIOUS"
Who are much too impatient to wait—
You have to believe in GOD'S PROMISE
That HE COMES NOT TOO SOON or TOO
        LATE,
For, whether GOD answers promptly
Or delays in answering your prayer,
YOU MUST HAVE FAITH TO BELIEVE HIM
And TO KNOW IN YOUR HEART HE'LL BE
        THERE . . .
So be not impatient or hasty,
Just TRUST in THE LORD and BELIEVE,
For whatever you ask in FAITH and LOVE
In abundance you are sure to RECEIVE.

Put Your Soul in God's Control

Many trials and troubles
Are scattered on our way,
Daily little crosses
Are a part of every day . . .
But the troubles we have suffered
Are over, passed, and through,
So why should bygone happenings
Keep on gravely troubling you . . .
And the problems that beset us
In the NOW and PRESENT HOUR
We need not try to solve alone
Without GOD'S GRACE and POWER
And those scheduled for tomorrow
Still belong to GOD ALONE—
They are still unborn and formless
And a part of the unknown . . .
So let us face the trouble
That is ours this present minute,
And count on GOD to help us
And put HIS MERCY in it
And forget the past and future
And dwell wholly on today,
For GOD controls the future
And HE will direct our way.

Prayers
Are the Stairs to God

Prayers are the stairs
We must climb every day,
If we would reach God
There is no other way,
For we learn to know God
When we meet Him in prayer
And ask Him to lighten
Our burden of care—
So start in the morning
And, though the way's steep,
Climb ever upward
'Til your eyes close in sleep—
For prayers are the stairs
That lead to the Lord,
And to meet Him in prayer
Is the climber's reward.

Somebody Loves You

SOMEBODY LOVES YOU more than you know,
SOMEBODY GOES WITH YOU wherever you go,
SOMEBODY REALLY and TRULY CARES
And LOVINGLY LISTENS TO ALL OF YOUR
      PRAYERS . . .
     Don't doubt for a minute
      that this is true,
     For GOD loves HIS CHILDREN
      and takes care of them, too . . .
     And all of HIS TREASURES
      are yours to share
     If you love HIM completely
      and show HIM you care . . .
     And if you "WALK IN HIS FOOTSTEPS"
      and have the FAITH to BELIEVE,
There's nothing you ask for
     that you will not receive!

10

My Garden of Prayer

For me, prayer is as simple as asking God for help and finding it, or telling Him what I need and feeling His Presence. I like the old hymn about the garden, where, "He walks with me and He talks with me, and He tells me I am His own . . . ." Here are some of the things I've found in my garden of prayer.

My garden beautifies my yard
     and adds fragrance to the air . . .
But it is also MY CATHEDRAL
     and MY QUIET PLACE OF PRAYER . . .
So little do we realize
     that "THE GLORY and THE POWER"
Of HE who made the UNIVERSE
     lies hidden in a flower.

And they heard the voice of the Lord God
walking in the garden in the cool of the day. . . .

Genesis 3:8

"Now I Lay Me Down to Sleep"

I remember so well this prayer I said
Each night as my Mother tucked me in bed.
And today this same prayer is still the best way
To "sign off with God" at the end of the day
And to ask Him your soul to safely keep
As you wearily close tired eyes in sleep
Feeling content that The Father Above
Will hold you secure in His great arms of love . . .
And having His promise that if ere you wake
His angels will reach down your sweet soul to take
Is perfect assurance that awake or asleep
God is always right there to tenderly keep
ALL of HIS CHILDREN ever SAFE in HIS CARE
For God's HERE and He's THERE and He's
      EVERYWHERE . . .
So into His hands each night as I sleep
I commit my soul for the dear Lord to keep
Knowing that if my soul should take flight
It will soar to "THE LAND WHERE THERE
      IS NO NIGHT."

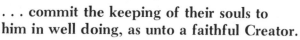

**. . . commit the keeping of their souls to
him in well doing, as unto a faithful Creator.**

1 Peter 4:19

Good Morning, God!

YOU are ushering in another day
Untouched and freshly new
So here I come to ask You, God,
If You'll renew me, too,
Forgive the many errors
That I made yesterday
And let me try again, dear God,
To walk closer in THY WAY . . .
But, Father, I am well aware
I can't make it on my own
So TAKE MY HAND and HOLD IT TIGHT
For I can't WALK ALONE!

. . . lo, I am with you alway. . . .

Matthew 28:20

"The House of Prayer"

"THE HOUSE OF PRAYER" is no farther away
Than the quiet spot where you kneel and pray,
For the heart is a temple when GOD is there
As you place yourself in HIS LOVING CARE.

Talk It Over With God

You're worried and troubled
    about everything,
Wondering and fearing
    what tomorrow will bring—
You long to tell someone
    for you feel so alone,
But your friends are all burdened
    with cares of their own—
There is only one place
    and only ONE FRIEND
Who is never too busy
    and you can always depend
That HE will be waiting
    with arms open wide
To hear all your troubles
    that you come to confide—
For the heavenly Father
    will always be there
When you seek HIM and find HIM
    at THE ALTAR of PRAYER.

**If any of you lack wisdom, let him ask of God . . .
and it shall be given him.**

James 1:5

The Heavenly Staircase

Prayers are the stairs that lead to God,
And there's joy every step of the way
When we make our pilgrimage to HIM
With love in our hearts each day.

He Answers All
Our Needs

There's no problem too big
       and no question too small,
Just ask GOD in FAITH
       and HE'LL answer them all—
Not always at once,
       so be patient and wait,
For "GOD never comes
       TOO SOON or TOO LATE—"
So trust in HIS WISDOM
       and believe in HIS WORD,
For no prayer's unanswered
       and no prayer unheard.

Call unto me, and I will answer thee. . . .
                                Jeremiah 33:3

Lives Distressed
Cannot Be Blessed

Refuse to be discouraged,
Refuse to be distressed,
For when we are despondent
Our life cannot be blessed—
For doubt and fear and worry
Close the door to FAITH and PRAYER,
For there's no room for blessings
When we're lost in deep despair—
So remember when you're troubled
With uncertainty and doubt
It is best to tell OUR FATHER
What our fear is all about—
For unless we seek His guidance
When troubled times arise
We are bound to make decisions
That are twisted and unwise—
But when we view our problems
Through the eyes of God above,
Misfortunes turn to blessings
And hatred turns to love.

**. . . the same Lord over all is rich
unto all that call upon him.**

                    Romans 10:12

Make It a
Two-Way Prayer

You're troubled and worried,
      you don't know what to do,
So you seek GOD in prayer
      and HE listens to you,
But you seldom pause
      to let GOD speak—
You just want the answer
      that you desperately seek . . .
And after you've pleaded,
      you don't give GOD a chance
To discuss the best way
      to meet your circumstance
And you really miss
      the best part of prayer—
Which is feeling and knowing
      GOD'S PRESENCE IS THERE . . .
For so few of us linger
      to quietly share
The "SILENT COMMUNION"
      that fills the air
In which GOD is speaking
      and telling us why
Sometimes there's no answer
      to our immediate cry . . .
So pause for a while
      and just silently wait
And give GOD a chance
      to communicate,
For TWO-WAY PRAYER
      forms a JOYOUS RELATION
When we listen to GOD
      in "SHARED MEDITATION."

Ask, and it shall be given you . . . .
              Matthew 7:7

A Special Prayer for You

Oh, Blessed Father, hear this prayer
     and keep all of us in Your care
Give us patience and inner sight, too,
     just as You often used to do
When on the shores of the Galilee
     You touched the blind and they could see
And cured the man who long was lame
     when he but called Your Holy Name!

You Are So Great . . .
     we are so small . . .
And when trouble comes
     as it does to us all
There's so little that we can do
     except to place our trust in You!

So take the Saviour's loving Hand
     and do not try to understand
Just let Him lead you where He will
     through "pastures green and waters still"
And place yourself in His loving care
     And He will gladly help you bear
Whatever lies ahead of you
     and God will see you safely through
And no earthly pain is ever too much
     if God bestows His merciful touch.

So I commend you into His care
     with a loving thought and a Special Prayer
And always remember, Whatever Betide You
     God is always beside you
And you cannot go beyond His love and care
     for we are all a part of God,
     and God is everywhere!

**. . . pray to thy Father which is in secret;
and thy Father which seeth in secret shall reward
thee openly.**

                              Matthew 6:6

11

Trust God's Plan

I have never had to worry about the future. Every time I have needed something, God has provided an answer—not always the answer I wanted—but as I look back, I can see that He has carried out a wise and beautiful plan. He will guide everyone who lets Him lead.

A Mother's Faith

It is a Mother's faith
    In our Father above
That fills the home with happiness
    And the heart with truth and love!

. . . he leadeth me . . . .

       Psalms 23:2

If We But Believe

If we put our problems in GOD'S HAND,
There is nothing we need understand . . .
It is enough to just believe
That what we need we will receive.

Humble yourselves therefore under the mighty
hand of God, that he may exalt you in due time:
Casting all your care upon him; for he careth for you.

1 Peter 5:6, 7

"In Him We Live, and Move, and Have Our Being"

We walk in a world that is strange and unknown
And in the midst of the crowd we still feel alone,
We question our purpose, our part and our place
In this vast land of mystery suspended in space,
We probe and explore and try hard to explain
The tumult of thoughts that our minds entertain . . .
But all of our probings and complex explanations
Of man's inner feelings and fears and frustrations
Still leave us engulfed in the "MYSTERY of LIFE"
With all of its struggles and suffering and strife,
Unable to fathom what tomorrow will bring—
But there is one truth to which we can cling,
For while LIFE'S a MYSTERY man can't understand
The "GREAT GIVER of LIFE" is holding our hand
And safe in HIS care there is no need for seeing
For "IN HIM WE LIVE and MOVE and HAVE OUR BEING."

Learn to Recognize
a Blessing

While it's very difficult
    for mankind to understand
GOD'S INTENTIONS and HIS PURPOSE
    and the WORKINGS of HIS HAND,
If we observe the miracles
    that happen every day,
We cannot help but be convinced
    that in HIS WONDROUS WAY
GOD makes what seemed unbearable
    and painful and distressing
Easily acceptable
    when we view it as a BLESSING.

What Is A Mother

It takes a Mother's Love to make a house
a home,
A place to be remembered,
no matter where we roam . . .
It takes a Mother's Patience
to bring a child
up right,
And her Courage and her Cheerfulness
to make a dark day bright . . .
It takes a Mother's Thoughtfulness
to mend the heart's deep "hurts",
And her Skill and her Endurance
to mend little socks
and shirts . . .
It takes a Mother's Kindness
to forgive us when we err
To sympathize in trouble
and bow her head in prayer . . .
It takes a Mother's Wisdom to recognize
our needs
And to give us reassurance
by her loving words
and deeds . . .
It takes a Mother's Endless Faith,
her Confidence and Trust
To guide us through the pitfalls
of selfishness
and lust . . .
And that is why in all this world
there could not be another
Who could fulfill God's purpose
as completely as
a Mother!

**When I call to remembrance the unfeigned faith
that is in thee, which dwelt first in thy grandmother
Lois, and thy mother Eunice . . . .**

2 Timothy 1:5

The Master Builder

GOD is THE MASTER BUILDER,
HIS PLANS are perfect and true,
And when HE sends you sorrow
It's part of HIS PLAN for you . . .
For all things work together
To complete THE MASTER PLAN
And GOD up in HIS HEAVEN
Can see what's best for man.

**And we know that all things work together
for good to them that love God . . . .**

Romans 8:28

God's Hand Is Always There

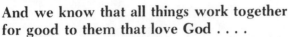

I am perplexed and often vexed
And sometimes I cry and sadly sigh,
But do not think, DEAR FATHER ABOVE,
I question YOU or YOUR UNCHANGING LOVE—
It's just sometimes when I reach out
YOU seem to be nowhere about . . .
And while I'm sure that YOU love me still
And I know in my heart that you ALWAYS WILL,
Somehow I feel that I cannot reach YOU
And though I get down on my knees and beseech YOU,
I cannot bring YOU closer to me
And I feel adrift on life's raging sea . . .
But though I cannot find YOUR HAND
To lead me on to THE PROMISED LAND,
I still believe with all my being
YOUR HAND IS THERE BEYOND MY SEEING!

Enfolded in His Love

The LOVE of GOD surrounds us
Like the air we breathe around us—
As near as a heartbeat,
     as close as a prayer,
And whenever we need HIM
      HE'LL always be there!

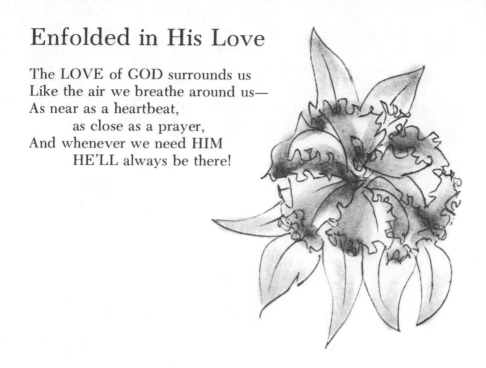

Trust and Believe
and You Will Receive

Whatever our problems, troubles, and sorrows,
If we trust in THE LORD, there'll be BRIGHTER TOMORROWS,
For there's nothing too much for THE GREAT GOD to do,
And all that HE asks or expects from you
Is FAITH that's unshaken by tribulations and tears
That keeps growing stronger along with the years,
Content in the knowledge that GOD knows best
And that trouble and sorrow are only a test—
For without GOD'S testing of our soul
It never would reach its ultimate goal . . .
So keep on believing, whatever betide you,
Knowing that GOD will be with you to guide you,
And all that HE PROMISED will be yours to receive
If you TRUST HIM COMPLETELY and ALWAYS BELIEVE.

. . . he hath said, I will never leave thee,
nor forsake thee.

Hebrews 13:5

My Daily Prayer

GOD, be MY RESTING PLACE and MY
      PROTECTION
In hours of trouble, defeat and dejection . . .
May I never give way to self-pity and sorrow,
May I always be sure of a better tomorrow,
May I stand undaunted come what may
Secure in the knowledge I have only to pray
And ask MY CREATOR and FATHER ABOVE
To keep me serene in HIS GRACE and HIS LOVE!

12
Thank You, God, for Everything

How many, many things there are for which to thank the Lord! These verses give only a hint of the countless reasons to be filled with praise and thanksgiving.

A Favorite Recipe

Take a CUP of KINDNESS,
        mix it well with LOVE,
Add a lot of Patience
        and FAITH in GOD ABOVE,
Sprinkle very generously
        with JOY and THANKS and CHEER—
And you'll have lots of "ANGEL FOOD"
        to feast on all the year.

Giving thanks always for all things . . . .

                        Ephesians 5:20

A Prayer of Thanks

Thank You, GOD, for everything
    I've experienced here on earth—
Thank You for protecting me
    from the moment of my birth—
And thank You for the beauty
    around me everywhere,
The gentle rain and glistening dew,
    the sunshine and the air,
The joyous gift of "feeling"
    the soul's soft, whispering voice
That speaks to me from deep within
    and makes my heart rejoice—
Oh, GOD, no words are great enough
    to thank You for just living,
And that is why every day
    is a day for real THANKSGIVING.

Every day will I bless thee . . . .

Psalms 145:2

Things to Be Thankful For

The good, green earth beneath our feet,
The air we breathe, the food we eat,
Some work to do, a goal to win,
A hidden longing deep within
That spurs us on to bigger things
And helps us meet what each day brings,
All these things and many more
Are things we should be thankful for . . .
And most of all our thankful prayers
Should rise to God because He cares!

A Thankful Heart

Take nothing for granted,
     for whenever you do
The "joy of enjoying"
     is lessened for you—
For we rob our own lives
     much more than we know
When we fail to respond
     or in any way show
Our thanks for the blessings
     that daily are ours . . .
The warmth of the sun,
     the fragrance of flowers,
The beauty of twilight,
     the freshness of dawn,
The coolness of dew
     on a green velvet lawn,
The kind little deeds
     so thoughtfully done,
The favors of friends
     and the love that someone
Unselfishly gives us
     in a myriad of ways,
Expecting no payment
     and no words of praise—
Oh, great is our loss
     when we no longer find
A thankful response
     to things of this kind,
For the Joy of Enjoying
     and the Fullness of Living
Are found in the heart that is
     filled with Thanksgiving.

Let us come before his presence with thanksgiving . . . .

Psalms 95:2

"I Meet God
In The Morning"

"The earth is the Lord's
          and the fulness thereof"—
It speaks of His greatness,
          it sings of His love,
And each day at dawning
          I lift my heart high
And raise up my eyes
          to the infinite sky . . .
I watch the night vanish
          as a new day is born,
And I hear the birds sing
          on the wings of the morn,
I see the dew glisten
          in crystal-like splendor
While God, with a touch
          that is gentle and tender,
Wraps up the night
          and softly tucks it away
And hangs out the sun
          to herald a new day . . .
And so I give thanks
          and my heart kneels to pray—
"God keep me and guide me
          and go with me today."

**. . . all the earth shall be filled
with the glory of the Lord.**

Numbers 14:21

Everywhere Across the Land
You See God's Face
And Touch His Hand

Each time you look up in the sky
Or watch the fluffy clouds drift by,
Or feel the sunshine warm and bright,
Or watch the dark night turn to light,
Or hear a bluebird gayly sing,
Or see the winter turn to spring,
Or stop to pick a daffodil,
Or gather violets on some hill,
Or touch a leaf or see a tree,
It's all God whispering, "This is Me . . .
And I am Faith and I am Light
And in Me there shall be No Night."

Wondrous Evidence

Who can see the dawn break through
        without a glimpse of HEAVEN and YOU . . .
For who but GOD could make the day
        and gently put the night away.

**The heavens declare the glory of God;
and the firmament sheweth his handywork.**

                        Psalms 19:1

So Many Reasons to Love the Lord

Thank You, God, for little things
      that come unexpectedly
To brighten up a dreary day
      that dawned so dismally—
Thank You, God, for sending
      a happy thought my way
To blot out my depression
      on a disappointing day—
Thank You, God, for brushing
      the "dark clouds" from my mind
And leaving only "sunshine"
      and joy of heart behind . . .
Oh, God, the list is endless
      of things to thank You for
But I take them all for granted
      and unconsciously ignore
That EVERYTHING I THINK or DO,
      each movement that I make,
Each measured rhythmic heartbeat,
      each breath of life I take
Is something You have given me
      for which there is no way
For me in all my "smallness"
      to in any way repay.

Showers of Blessings

Each day
there are showers of blessings
sent from the Father Above,
For God is a great, lavish giver
and there is no end to His love—
His grace
is more than sufficient,
His mercy is boundless and deep,
And His infinite blessings
are countless
and all this we're given to keep,
If we but seek God
and find Him
and ask for a bounteous measure
Of this wholly immeasurable offering
from God's inexhaustible treasure—
For no matter
how big man's dreams are,
God's blessings are Infinitely more,
For always God's Giving
is greater
than what man is Asking for.

13
Life Can't Always Be a Song

I have always had a pretty strong constitution, and most of my life, I've been blessed with excellent health. But in recent years I have found myself at times in a sickbed or hospital. When I had to spend one birthday in a hospital, I wrote about it in the poem, "My Birthday in Bethesda."

Life can't always be a song, but even our troubles can work for us, if we let go and let God work through them.

Life Can't Always Be a Song—
You Have to Have Trouble
to Make You Strong . . .

So whenever you are troubled
And everything goes wrong,
It is just GOD working in you
To make YOUR SPIRIT STRONG!

Yea, a sword shall pierce through thy own soul . . .
[Simeon speaking to Mary the Mother].

Luke 2:35

My Birthday in Bethesda

How little we know what GOD has in store
As daily HE blesses our lives more and more . . .
I've lived many years and learned many things,
But today I have grown "NEW SPIRITUAL
    WINGS,"
For pain has a way of broadening our view
And bringing us closer in sympathy, too,
To those who are living in constant pain
And trying somehow to bravely sustain
The faith and endurance to keep on trying
When they almost welcome "the peace of dying" . . .
And without this experience I would have lived
    and died
Without fathoming the pain of CHRIST crucified,
For none of us know what pain's all about
Until our "SPIRITUAL WINGS" start to sprout . . .
So thank YOU, GOD, for the "GIFT" YOU sent
To teach me that pain is HEAVEN-SENT.

**More than that, we rejoice in our sufferings,
knowing that suffering produces endurance, and endurance
produces character . . . .**

Romans 5:3, 4 RSV

Sorrow Helps
Our Souls to Grow

There's a lot of comfort in the thought
That sorrow, grief, and woe
Are sent into our lives sometimes
To help our souls to grow . . .
For through the depths of sorrow
Comes understanding love,
And peace and truth and comfort
Are sent from GOD ABOVE.

God, Are You There?

I'm way down HERE!
You're way up THERE!
Are You sure You can hear
My faint, faltering prayer?
For I'm so unsure
Of just how to pray—
To tell you the truth, God,
I don't know what to say . . .
I just know I am lonely
And vaguely disturbed,
Bewildered and restless,
Confused and perturbed . . .
And they tell me that prayer
Helps to quiet the mind
And to unburden the heart
For in stillness we find
A newborn assurance
That SOMEONE DOES CARE
And SOMEONE DOES ANSWER
Each small sincere prayer!

**Be still, and know that I
am God . . . .**

Psalms 46:10

Blessings in Disguise Are Difficult to Recognize

God sends His "little angels"
        in many forms and guises,
They come as lovely miracles
        that God alone devises—
For He does nothing without purpose,
        everything's a perfect plan
To fulfill in bounteous measure
        all He ever promised man—
For every "little angel"
        with a body bent and broken,
Or a little mind retarded
        or little words unspoken,
Is just God's way of trying
        to reach and touch the hand
Of all who do not know Him
        and cannot understand
That often through an angel
        whose "wings will never fly"
The Lord is pointing out the way
        to His eternal sky
Where there will be no handicaps
        of body, soul or mind,
And where all limitations
        will be dropped and left behind—
So accept these "little angels"
        as gifts from God above
And thank Him for this lesson
        in FAITH and HOPE and LOVE.

How Little We Know
of Suffering and Woe

GOD, how little I was really aware
Of the pain and the trouble and deep despair
That floods the hearts of those in pain
As they struggle to cope but feel it's in vain,
Crushed with frustration and with "no haven to seek,"
With broken spirits and bodies so weak . . .
And yet they forget CHRIST suffered and died
And hung on the cross and was crucified,
And HE did it all so some happy day,
When the sorrows of earth have all passed away,
We who have suffered will forever be free
To live with GOD in ETERNITY!

Today, Tomorrow, and
Always He Is There

In sickness or health,
In suffering and pain,
In storm-laden skies,
In sunshine and rain,
GOD ALWAYS IS THERE
To lighten your way
And lead you through "darkness"
To a much brighter day.

A Time of Renewal and Spiritual Blessing

No one likes to be sick
     and yet we know
It takes sunshine and rain
     to make flowers grow . . .
And if we never were sick
     and never felt pain,
We'd be like a desert
     without any rain,
And who wants a life
     that is barren and dry
With never a "cloud"
     to "darken the sky" . . .
For "continuous sun"
     goes unrecognized
Like the blessings GOD sends
     which are often disguised,
For sometimes a sickness
     that seems so distressing
Is a "time of renewal"
     and a "spiritual blessing."

He maketh me to lie down . . . . He restoreth my soul . . . .

Psalms 23:2, 3

Are You Physically Ill or Soul Sick?

Sometimes when we are
    physically ill
We're prone to resort
    to a tonic or pill,
Neglecting to place
    ourselves in GOD'S CARE
By seeking HIS help
    on "THE WINGS OF PRAYER"—
For GOD can remove
    our uncertain fear
And replace our worry
    with healing cheer . . .
So close your eyes
    and open your heart
And let GOD come in
    and freely impart
A brighter outlook
    and new courage, too,
As HIS "spiritual sunshine"
    smiles on you.

Why Am I Complaining?

My cross is not too heavy,
My road is not too rough
Because God walks beside me
And to know this is enough . . .
And though I get so lonely
I know I'm not alone
For the Lord God is my Father
And He loves me as His own . . .
So though I'm tired and weary
And I wish my race were run
God will only terminate it
When my work on earth is done . . .
So let me stop complaining
About my "LOAD of CARE"
For God will always lighten it
When it gets too much to bear . . .
And if He does not ease my load
He will give me strength to bear it
For God in love and mercy
Is always near to share it.

When thou passest through the waters,
I will be with thee;
and through the rivers,
they shall not overflow thee:
when thou walkest through the fire,
thou shalt not be burned . . . .

Isaiah 43:2

Nothing on Earth is Forever Yours—
Only the Love of the Lord Endures!

Everything in life is passing
     and whatever we possess
Cannot endure forever
     but ends in nothingness,
For there are no safety boxes
     nor vaults that can contain
The possessions we collected
     and desire to retain . . .
So all that man acquires,
     be it power, fame or jewels,
Is but limited and earthly,
     only "treasure made for fools" . . .
For only in GOD'S KINGDOM
     can man find enduring treasure,
Priceless gifts of love and beauty—
     more than mortal man can measure,
And the "riches" he accumulates
     he can keep and part with never,
For only in GOD'S KINGDOM
     do our treasures last FOREVER . . .
So use the word FOREVER
     with sanctity and love,
For NOTHING IS FOREVER
     BUT THE LOVE OF GOD ABOVE!

14

The End of the Road
Is But a Bend in the Road

As the years fly swiftly by, all of us may well wonder what the future holds in store for us. But experience shows that what looks like the end of the road is really only a bend in the road! This was brought home to me when my own dear mother left my sister and me for the regions beyond. I wrote the poem "My Mother's Message to Me" right after her death. It expresses her faith that we will be together again up above.

Where this life ends, eternal life begins. Death opens the door to Life Evermore!

●

God's Mighty Handiwork

"The earth is THE LORD'S
    and the fulness thereof"—
It speaks of HIS GREATNESS
    and it sings of HIS LOVE—
It whispers of mysteries
    we cannot comprehend
Of a beautiful land
    where life has no end!

In the Hands of God
Even Death Is
a Time for Rejoicing

And so when death brings weeping
      and the heart is filled with sorrow,
It beckons us to seek GOD
      as we ask about "TOMORROW" . . .
And in these hours of "heart-hurt"
      we draw closer to believing
That even death in GOD'S HANDS
      is not a cause for grieving
But a time for joy in knowing
      death is just a stepping-stone
To a LIFE that's EVERLASTING
      such as we have never known.

Fear thou not; for I am with thee . . . .

Isaiah 41:10

There's Always
a Springtime

After the Winter comes the Spring
To show us again that in everything
There's always renewal divinely planned,
Flawlessly perfect, the work of God's Hand . . .
And just like the seasons that come and go
When the flowers of Spring lay buried in snow,
God sends to the heart in its winter of sadness
A springtime awakening of new hope and gladness,
And loved ones who sleep in a season of death
Will, too, be awakened by God's life-giving breath.

Jesus said unto her, I am the resurrection, and the life:
he that believeth in me, though he were dead, yet shall he live:
And whosoever liveth and believeth in me shall never die . . . .

John 11:25, 26

My Mother's Message to Me

When I must leave you for a little while
Please do not grieve and shed wild tears
And hug your sorrow to you through the years,
But start out bravely with a gallant smile;
And for my sake and in my name
Live on and do all things the same,
Feed not your loneliness on empty days
But fill each waking hour in useful ways,
Reach out your hand in comfort and in cheer
And I in turn will comfort you and hold you near,
And never, never be afraid to die
For I am waiting for you in the sky!

In my Father's house are many mansions . . . .

John 14:2

The End of the Road
Is but a Bend in the Road

When we feel
we have nothing left to give
And we are sure
that the "song has ended"—
When our day seems over
and the shadows fall
And the darkness of night has descended,
Where can we go to find the strength
To valiantly keep on trying,
Where can we find the hand that will dry
The tears that the heart is crying—
There's but one place to go
and that is to God
And, dropping all pretense and pride,
We can pour out our problems
without restraint
And gain strength with Him at our side—
And together we stand at life's crossroads
And view what we think is the end,
But God has a much bigger vision
And He tells us it's Only a Bend—
For the road goes on
and is smoother,
And the "pause in the song"
is a "rest,"
And the part that's unsung
and unfinished
Is the sweetest and richest
and best—
So rest and relax and grow stronger,
Let Go and Let God
share your load,
Your work is not finished or ended,
You've just come to
"A Bend In The Road."

**Surely goodness and mercy shall follow
me all the days of my life: and I will dwell
in the house of the Lord for ever.**

Psalms 23:6

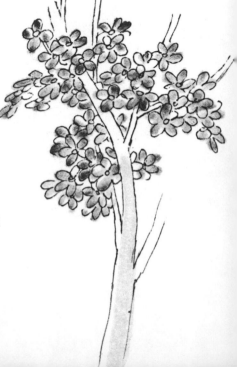

Listen With Your Heart

Memories are a treasure
        time cannot take away . . .
So may you be surrounded
        by happy ones today . . .
May all the love and tenderness
        of golden years well spent
Come back today to fill your heart
        with beauty and content . . .
And may you walk down MEMORY LANE
        and meet the one you love
For while you cannot see him,
        he'll be watching from above . . .
And if you trust your dreaming
        your faith will make it true . . .
And if you listen with your heart
        he'll come and talk with you . . .
So for his sake be happy
        and show him that his love
Has proven strong and big enough
        to reach down from above . . .
And you will never walk alone
        when Memory's Door swings wide . . .
For you'll find that your beloved
        is always at your side.

**And this is the promise that he hath promised
us, even eternal life.**

                      1 John 2:25

Death Is a Doorway

On the "WINGS of DEATH"
    the "SOUL takes FLIGHT"
Into the land where
    "THERE IS NO NIGHT"—
For those who believe
    what the Saviour said
Will rise in glory
    though they be dead . . .
So death comes to us
    just to "OPEN the DOOR"
To the KINGDOM of GOD
    and LIFE EVERMORE.

For to me to live is Christ, and to die is gain.

Philippians 1:21

I Do Not Go Alone

If Death should beckon me
with outstretched hand
And whisper softly of "An Unknown Land" . . .
I shall not be
afraid to go,
For though the path I do not know,
I take Death's Hand
without a fear,
For He who safely brought me here
Will also take me
safely back,
And though in many things I lack,
He will not let me
go alone
Into the "Valley That's Unknown" . . .
So I reach out
and take Death's Hand
And journey to the "Promised Land!"

"Because He Lives . . .
We Too Shall Live"

In this restless world of struggle
    It is very hard to find
Answers to the questions
    That daily come to mind—
We cannot see the future,
    What's beyond is still unknown,
For the secret of God's Kingdom
    Still belongs to Him alone—
Bue He granted us salvation
    When His Son was crucified,
For life became immortal
    Because our Saviour died.

Life Is Forever!
Death Is a Dream!

If we did not go to sleep at night
We'd never awaken to see the light,
And the joy of watching
    a new day break
Or meeting the dawn
    by some quiet lake
Would never be ours unless we slept
While God and all His angels kept
A vigil through this "little death"
That's over with the morning's breath—
And death, too, is a time of sleeping,
    For those who die
    are in God's keeping
And there's a "sunrise" for each soul,
    For LIFE not DEATH
    is God's promised goal—
    So trust God's promise
    and doubt Him never
    For only through death
    can man LIVE FOREVER!

Mothers Never Really Die—
They Just Keep House Up in the Sky

Death beckoned her with outstretched hand
And whispered softly of "An Unknown Land"—
But she was not afraid to go
For though the path she did not know,
She took Death's Hand without a fear,
For He who safely brought her here
Had told her He would lead the way
Into Eternity's Bright Day . . .
And so she did not go alone
Into the "Valley That's Unknown"—
She gently took Death By the Hand
And journeyed to "The Promised Land" . . .
And there, with step so light and gay,
She polishes the sun by day
And lights the stars that shine at night
And keeps the moonbeams silvery bright . . .
For Mothers really never die,
They just "Keep House Up In The Sky" . . .
And in the Heavenly Home Above
They wait to "welcome" those they love.

**And the world passeth away . . . but he
that doeth the will of God abideth for ever.**

1 John 2:17